MW01603102

Night and Light
and
the Half-light

poems by
Henry George Fischer

Pocahontas Press, Inc.
Blacksburg, Virginia

ACKNOWLEDGMENTS
(referring to pages)

The Lyric: 3, 4, 5, 6, 7, 11, 14, 17, 20, 23t, 28, 43, 47t, 52, 53, 68, 72
Light Quarterly: 30, 32, 33 (with translation), 35t, 37, 39b, 40b, 42, 45
ELF: Eclectic Literary Forum: 23b, 24, 29, 34, 39t, 40t
Studies in Contemporary Satire: 31, 33, 38, 41, 46
Piedmont Literary Review: 2, 64–65, 67, 74
American Poets and Poetry: 10, 12, 19, 54–55
Candelabrum: 18, 21, 22, 62
Sparrow: 1, 15, 48, 59
Poetry Digest: 9, 60–61, 70, 71
Midwest Poetry Review: 8, 44, 49   *Orbis:* 63
The Classical Outlook: 35b, 36   *Poetpourri:* 25
Comstock Poetry Review: 56, 58   *Poetry:* 16
Troubadour: 66, 73   *RE Arts and Letters:* 51
Byline: 27   *Shakespeare Newsletter:* 69
The Epigrammatist: 47b   *Sherman Sentinel:* 26
Hellas: 50   *The Tennessee Quarterly:* 57

A Light Calendar for 1998: 32
Random House Treasury of Light Verse: 25, 45
The Red Candle Treasury: 13, 63
This Is the Town I Remember, ed. Wilson Ware: 26

Manufactured in the United States of America and published by
Pocahontas Press, P.O. Drawer F, Blacksburg, Virginia 24063–1020
Typeset in New Baskerville by Peter Der Manuelian, Boston Massachusetts
Designed by the author and Peter Der Manuelian

ISBN 0–936015–79–9

To Katherine

A poem
More to be admired
Than any other
I have sired

Contents

Night

Light

The Half-light

All Souls' Day

BENEATH their sundry stones, locked under rock,
The dead lie still, and so they will until
Someone comes by who can turn back the clock
Of memory, and charm them from their chill.

Beneath those numbing stones their tongues are dumb
Unless we hear them echo in the mind.
If now we grant them a chrysanthemum,
It isn't to delight them; they are blind.

It's that this flower, defying frosts of fall,
May waken what's in us of what they were,
A flower that has the power to recall
Them from forgetfulness, that murderer.

And as we think of them we think they've stirred
And spoken to us. Listen ! Mum's the word.

Like a Rhyme

Jadis déjà !
Verlaine

WE'RE scarcely severed by the midwife's knife,
And snatched from slumbers plumblessly sublime,
We've hardly howled and hurtled into life,
When, like a rhyme, we are recalled by time.

We cannot linger, longing for what's lost,
Now we are past our best, and down we climb
Until we're old and mouldy, sadly mossed,
And like a rhyme, long since recalled by time.

Though we recall a time when, like a rhyme,
Our days delighted and our nights were rocked
In sleep unreckoned as a paradigm,
Now we're rheumatic, restless, and we're mocked
By all the aching hours since our first breath.
Our debt to time is called; it rhymes with death.

The Nightingale

I PICTURE Keats as one whose look was pale
When, with a faint forefeeling of his end,
He failed to hear the vanished nightingale.
Sounds, savours, sights and scents would send
Through him a pang that passioned him to sing,
Yet sing in sadness that they are but brief,
And being brief, such joys can only bring
All mortals to the ground of all their grief.

And how short were his joys, though he enlisted
All his senses to prolong their measure,
And how he sang of them, how he insisted
On both notes of a sadly passing pleasure.

How soon, a songbird to a small cell banished
Beside the Spanish Steps, he also vanished.

Rest In Print

WHEN I am dead, I'll not be found
Beneath a stone, but I'll be bound
You will not have so far to look,
For I'll be buried in a book;

A book whose type displays the skill
And mastery of Baskerville;
Whose paper is quite acid-free,
Its signatures sewn tidily

Between stout boards and clad in cloth
That tames the tooth of worm and moth.
I can't think where I'd rather be
When words are all that's left of me.

And any corpse, in such a tomb,
Is such a pleasure to exhume !

May and Dismay

THE winds no longer are at war,
And last year's leaves, turned turtle,
Find final footing on a forest floor
Patched, purpled now with myrtle.

Peopled with piping birds, the trees renew
Their limbs, so lightly laced with leaves
They scarcely screen with green the blue
Above. All this repairs, reprieves,

All this of May repays for many days
Of darkness, snow and sleet.
With joy I now rejoin it and I greet;
And yet dismay comes over me and weighs
With all the freight of so much age
As brings a winter no spring can assuage.

Let Your Cup be Full

O LET your cup be full until it spills;
Let every tumbling stream become a torrent,
A stream that freely flows until it mills
And multiplies into a cresting current.

Let brimming brooks, unbridled, have their way,
And words their wayward will, that they may be
Poured, stirred in everything you sing and say
Till, like those waters, you have found the sea.

Then, guided by the tidings of the ocean,
You'll feel its sway in every syllable,
And all the rolling waters in their motion
Will find them full and ever fillable.

O have your fill of it before you drain
Into the dust that is death's dry domain.

Motes

WHEN I was young, was very young,
Motes, caught within a straying ray
Of sunlight, carried me away;
 I hung upon them as they hung.

Miniscule moons they were, which floated
Airborne, heedless that they must,
Like all motes, join their mates as dust,
A consequence I little noted.

How well I picture how it was;
Time, like motes, then seemed suspended,
Buoyed by currents, was upended.

Now I'm old, it will not pause
But settles on me; I'm aghast
To find dust deepening so fast.

Circe

Is WHAT they say of Circe true
Or only hearsay ? If I knew,
Would I risk my skin to visit
Her, to win her wine ? And is it
Not the case she'd lay me low,
Before I downed it to the dregs,
So low I'd be compelled to go
Upon all fours, a thing that begs
The scraps she condescends to throw ?

If she flickered her fingers at me,
Would I not turn tail and flee
Upon my hands and feet turned paws,
And find my raucous voice a maw
Instead of mouth, to caterwaul
The ignominy of my fell and fall ?

How can she, even in our sleep,
So hold our sinking thoughts in thrall
That we would risk our flesh to creep,
That we'd resign to her our skin to crawl ?

Perilous Seas

SOME seek the Land of Cockaigne with cocaine,
Or other regions that are transmundane.
Some empty time till it's but an abyss,
Infantilized by fumes of cannabis.
Or take unchartered trips with LSD
In hope of ending up in ecstasy.
While others dream with drugs by which they sleep;
And thereby climb to heights or plumb the deep.

The other side of anywhere but this
Is where they fare to find their share of bliss.
But who can say what fartherness they win,
When all their otherness is found within ?
Though they sail perilous seas, few of their feats
Are logged save those of Coleridge and of Keats.

Poets of the Past

THE troubled tributaries of my life
Now run their course and seam a sea of silence,
A slumbrous sea, on which one fallen leaf
Repeats another, and those fragile islands
Are my thoughts, which fleeting, float away.
Can I find syllables to sail with them,
Find words to work their way where none will stay,
Or pace their passage with a palsied pen ?

Only the dead have power to move my lips,
To prompt my pen, to find my failing voice
Its fill of wind to wing those spindling ships,
And home them to the harbor of my choice.

Immortal ports of poets who are gone,
You beacon me, a pale ephemeron.

Wizardry

If I were master of this wizardry,
I'd catch you by catoptric tricks and tropes,
I would, behind a mirrored vizard, be
Invisible; with mirrored telescopes
I'd bring the uttermost of outer space
Into your somnolence, that in those seas
Your eyes would wander where the pale stars pace,
Would riddle all the skies' eternities.

Meanwhile, with meaner mirrors, I would wink
Things out of sight, twist, convolute, transmute;
Bring fleeting, flickering visions to the brink
Of being, posed, poised, irresolute.

And you who gazed, dazed by my mirrors' beams
Would be mirabilized by mirrored dreams.

The Exile

PERHAPS by now, he does not often think
About his family's ravaged olive groves,
The empty well from which they used to drink,
For even when unthought of, such things chafe,
Nor does he like to think of what he owes
The cold collaboration of his foes.

Though sometimes haunted by a loss of *kayf*,
A feeling of repose when rest was sought,
And, in this land of plenty, can't be bought
And cannot be recovered by belief;
I've seen and felt the sources of his grief.

And see his shadow where I once saw mine,
Upon the stricken soil of Palestine.

Pepys Courts Catherine of Valois

I had the upper part of her body in my hands, and I did kiss her
mouth, reflecting upon it that I did kiss a Queen and that this was
my birth-day, thirty-six years old....
Diary, February 23, 1669

DID Pepys' presumptuous heart not start to skip
When he embraced the wasted corpse of Kate ?
Did he, before he dared to put his lip.
Where lipless teeth were bared, not hesitate
To be so bold, draw back and hold his breath ?
Was he made bold to think he'd reached her age
That day, recorded on his diary's page,
Since she was six and thirty at her death ?

Two centuries and more had come between
Them though, when in that fine and private place
Where none, as Marvell noted, do embrace,
He flirted on his birthday with a queen.

And Marvell, twelve years wiser, might have shuddered
To think Pepys had rebutted what he'd uttered !

Goodbyes

How longingly they look who know
They are but guests, and they must go,
For no one can, without a sigh,
See the last of, say goodbye

To anything, except for pain;
We miss what will not come again,
And even what's today a sorrow
May be yearned for come tomorrow.

It's not simply that one clings
To people, places, or to things;
We may forego, we may forget,
But all farewells entail regret.

Indeed you hope this may be true
For those who've seen the last of *you*.

Sonnet on Tennyson

Dear mother Ida, harken ere I die.
Oenone

HE WAS a master of chiasmus,
Spanning chasms of miasmas,
Rhyming rosaries of sorrow
With a rumor of tomorrow.

And how mortal that tomorrow,
And how dolorous that sorrow !
Through his head and heart and torso
Sorrow's morrows flowed the more so.

Isn't all that's human doomed ?
Is it still human when inhumed ?
Equivocal soliloquies
Left him bereft by thoughts like these.

He groped his way along a swaying rope
That risked the distance between here and hope.

The Closet-drinker

How the glee ran out of his face
The day his cellar went dry at last !
The corks lay all about the place,
Dead bottles so thick we couldn't get past.

His soul, a delicate corkscrew,
Inhabited every glass he lipped;
How it would give him a turn if he knew
That we'd turned his cellar into a crypt !

How the wine ran out of his veins
The day we laid him in that well
Of a cellar ! Now nothing remains
Of the house, in the flooded crypt where it fell.

Between

WE STAND between a fiery core
We hope won't burn us any more
And a big fire in the sky
On whose burning we rely.

The pair of planets we're between is
Kept at odds by Mars and Venus;
And the nearer sway of Mars
Keeps us in the midst of wars.

We live on islands between oceans,
Which the moon moves in its motions.
Our passions swing twixt love and hate,
Whose tidings dominate our fate.

We are vexed to be betwixt
And not to know what's coming next;
Between the future and the past
Our optimism's at half-mast.

Our hands are fumbling at the ropes
That are the halyards of our hopes;
We tug the bootstraps of belief,
But cannot get us off our reef,

A reef that's rife with strife, a strand
That is itself twixt sea and land.

A Dry Season

Quand tonneras-tu, foudre ?
Baudelaire

THERE is a tingling in my bones;
Far off the hoarse voice of a train
Rehearses a forgotten pain,
And chirring locusts, to my ears,
Insist like distant telephones
Or like a shivering of shears.

The sky is mumbling now in lieu
Of torrents that are overdue,
And while indoors I'm tricked by drops
That drain from driveling watercocks,

When will I ever hear again
A proud cloud, racked with thunder,
With birth-pangs, split itself and sunder
As it's delivered of its brood of rain ?

A Return

IT IS the very old, the very young
Who dote most on the echoes words may make
When tripped on lips or tumbled on the tongue;
They tease young hearts, and later ease their ache.

The old, their middle years obliterated,
Hark metrically back to seesaws, swings,
A time when weightless words, alliterated
Or rhymed, endowed their waking wits with wings;

It is as if they've learnt to talk again.
And so the old, when they've retraced their traces
Past platitudes of a prosaic plain,
May find a font of youth in an oasis:

For some a mere mirage, a mirrored shimmer,
Yet it grows brighter as their eyes grow dimmer.

De la Musique avant Toute Chose

How many poems cannot find any homes;
How many winged words, still on the wing,
Hover in holding flight while poedromes
Deny them space to give them harboring.

How many tongues are tied, too tired to tell
Of anything that stirred their words to flight
Because their words found nowhere they might dwell,
And they could not invade where none invite.

How few have ears that still will hear a lyric,
Or voice a verse instead of merely reading,
Or even mutter metre that's satyric;
How seldom lips accede to metre's leading.

As he who's heeded me thus far well knows,
The poems we prize are muzzled, puzzled prose.

To a Superior Sonneteer

I CANNOT match you, cannot light a match
That's light enough; I cannot hold a candle
To your sonnets, and can only dandle
Words like these. My candle's but a patch
Of glimmer that's put out by so much brightness,
Like glow-worms that, more cunning, sleep by day
Because they know their lamps will fade to gray,
Or dun, undone by dint of daylight's whiteness.

And yet, like you, I feel the sway of words
That waken us to what is dreamt within
And carry us away like bursts of birds
Or flying fish that plunge with flashing fin.

Ah yes, we are seduced by the same spell,
But if it cannot kindle, it will quell.

Witches

Vous que dans votre enfer mon âme a poursuivies,
Pauvres soeurs, je vous aime autant que je vous plains
Baudelaire

THOSE spectral sisters, with their potent potions,
Impelled their brittle bones to farther flights
Than ever marvelled at. The skies and oceans
Were equally their element, for heights
And depths alike excited their desires,
However drunk with air, however drenched
With wanton waters; all winds fanned their fires,
Which roiled the seas and still were never quenched.

A far cry from the crones that once they were,
They soared or plunged triumphant, newly limbed,
Resurgent, skin refulgent, with their hair
Coiled all about them gleaming, never dimmed.

Dementedly they sped astride the night
To sound the steep, the deep dimensions of delight.

Mayonnaise

It is the amphiphilic properties of lecithin in egg
yolk that enable aqueous vinegar to emulsify with
the vegetable oil in mayonnaise.
                                        M.D. Magazine

WOULDN'T life be more idyllic
If we could be amphiphilic ?
If we all became emulsive,
None would ever seem repulsive;
In one melting pot we'd mix
Until we found that no one sticks.
Then, instead of wine or gin,
We'd drink our healths in lecithin,
And life would be, through all our days,
Just a bowl of mayonnaise.

The Frog Declines a Kiss

I FEAR thy lips, bewitching wench,
And what they may forebode;
I'd rather be a loveless frog
Than be a Liebes-toad.

A Song of Seduction,
in Three Voices

HE SLYLY sidled to her side;
Her palate and her ear were plied
With serenades and lemonade,
All to belie the plot he laid.

With syrupy and scented sweets,
And oft-repeated soft conceits,
His syllables, like sillabubs,
Reduced her stubborness to stubs.

His wiles were such she was beguiled,
One wile away from being defiled,
When she, before she had concurred,
Beneath his false falsetto heard,
In tones low-keyed but eloquent,
The tenor of his bass intent.

Henry VIII

WHEN he decreed
He'd be rewedded,
They had to heed
Or be beheaded.

He lost his head
To Anne Boleyn,
He his who said
It was a sin.

"No more, no more !
Sir Thomas cried,
"No more of More !"
The king replied.

It's sad,
But if More *had*
Had more success,
We never would have had
Queen Bess.

Typo

By a slip of the pen
(Yours, not mine)
You've changed Madeleine
To Madeline.

I hope it isn't by design
That you've reduced
To Madeline
The dreams of Proust.

For if from Madeleine you take
Her due of e's,
She is dis-eased, a stomach-cake
To tease his teas.

So take back Madeline
(She's yours, not mine).
Give us again
Our Madeleine !

Typos

How bugged I am by disappointment
When a fly is in my ointment.
Were I an entomologist,
I'd spot it sooner, and not later,
Or it would simply not exist
Were I a pest-exterminator.

This is, alas, a kind of fly
No fisher ever wants to ply,
Although he might anoint his fly
With wax, perhaps, to keep it dry,
So lightly floating on the current
That it seemed as if it weren't.

What mine might catch he'd hardly wish:
A reader's eye, but not a fish.

The Loves of Jupiter

I KNOW of few girls stupider
Than Io, cowed by Jupiter.
(And it seems quite preposterous
That she should name the Bosphorus.)

Or Leda, who is such a goose
As anybody might seduce,
For Jupiter has but to don
Some feathers, and she sees a swan.

Semele's unseemly plea
To view him in his majesty
Is well repaid, for only dolts
Would go to bed with thunderbolts.

Though it is just mythology,
Callisto's lame apology
To vexed Diana puzzles me:
She claims that she thought he was she !

And as for Danaë, she's sold
On having sex with bags of gold,
In consequence of which, she nurses
No other progeny but Perseus.

The Proudest Pyramid

The proudest pyramid of them all, which
wealth and science have erected, has lost
its apex, and stands obtruncated in the
traveller's horizon.
Laurence Sterne

THE tomb of Cheops has no peer amid
The pyramids, though we have pity on
It when, should its tip not be hid
By clouds, we find no pyramidion,

Nor, if we enter it and look inside,
Can we find hair of him or any hide.
Yet neither of these facts this fact forbids:
It has no peer amid the pyramids.

Some say, because its limestone casing's
Also lost, it's self-effacing.
And, unless you save the surface,
You lose all, and it is worthless.

But even so, divested of veneer,
Apex and occupant, it has no peer.

Ozymandias à la Velikovsky

Two vast and trunkless legs might represent
A very arguable elephant;
Though some may say the proof of such a beast
Requires four vast and trunkless legs at least.

But if you search the sand a little deeper,
You'll find the shattered visage of his keeper,
A man who couldn't keep his head, perhaps,
When he beheld the elephant's collapse.

It's true that some have said, and all repeat,
That, written on the base beneath the feet
Of those two legs, so vast, though lacking knees,
There was a statement signed by Ramesses.

But that's no proof, because that boastful king
Contrived to put his name on everything,
Erasing any trace or smell or scent
That might bear witness to an elephant.

A Funny Pleasure Dome
with Caves of Mice

It was an Abyssinian cat,
And on a dulcimer she sat,
But when she hears it played she struts,
Its strings atingle in her guts.

Like any cat that has a home,
She takes it for her pleasure dome;
She walks according to her notion,
Meandering with a mazy motion.

Had I in me her tympani of purring,
I'd sleep away my days, unstirring,
And weave in sinuous circles thrice
A night before the caves of mice.

Then all within, eyes closed with dread,
Would listen for my stealthy tread,
And all who heard would tremble at
The honeyed mew of Kubla Cat !

Bored

HE WAS bored, but not with standing;
Notwithstanding, he was bored.

Too often, when he got to sit, he
Got to sit on a committee.
That is what he found a bore.

Those he sat with weren't appealing:
They would simply hit the ceiling
If they couldn't get the floor.

He tried to sit it out but swore
He couldn't stand it anymore.

Le Malheur du Mallarméen

La chair est triste, hélas

LA CHÈRE aussi; elle lasse,
Elle n'est plus grasse.

C'est très bien pour la santé, mais
Pourtant, je m'en sens mal-armé.

Mallarmé Inspires Some Alarm

The flesh is sad, alas

NO FLESH now; we've but fowl and fish,
Which have less fat than one might wish.

I'm sure much health and little harm may
Come of this, yet some alarm may.

De Sade

IT'S SAID de Sade
Could be a masochist;
Though that seems odd,
Such things may coexist.

And it would give him pause
Sometimes, twixt dusk and dawn,
To know which Sade he was,
And which side he was on.

Who knows what did
Decide de Sade
To make his id
Play martyr or play God ?

Priorities

IT SEEMS peculiar that our cat
Mews only when she wants a pat,
Whereas her plea is mute, not mewed,
Whenever she's in need of food.

Aren't her priorities reversed
By putting tactile pleasures first ?
Or do you think this rather tends
To show she loves food less than friends ?

For my part, I believe the latter;
So when I hear her mew, I pat her.

Phidias

IT WAS perfidious of Pericles to fail
To keep poor Phidias from rotting in the jail
In which he finally perished of disease.
The moral of all stories such as these
Is to abhor all patrons in high places.
But that depends a lot on what our case is,
For we can't always do just as we please !

Modern Verse
(Viewed from the Netherworld)

Though here on earth I hear few voices
Voice such poems as are my choices,
Should those voices not concern us
That are yearning in Avernus ?

"This verse," says poor Persephone,
"Will be the final death of me;
I cannot wait for Ceres,
It so winters me and wearies !"

"I'm sure," retorts Euridice,
"I don't know what *I* did to see
Such stuff; I look for Orpheus,
And find no more than Morpheus !"

Their plaint, at bottom, has such merit
That I'm stirred to disinter it.

Adam's Rib

WHEN he was first created, Adam
Was neither sir nor was he madam.
For only when decostalated
Could his sex be clearly stated.

Then only did his yang begin
To feel the pang of a yen for yin;
Adam felt ribald without that rib,
Which was also the start of women's lib.

How fortunate it was, and fitting
That God should practice Adam-splitting,
Out of which He cannily
Produced the nuclear family.

Yet who'd suppose, when God resects
A rib, there'd be such side-effects !

Kyrielle

LAUGHING off his marriage vow
He pushed his wife in a canal
But she was a *femme fatale,*
And who laughs now ?
Oui, qui rit ? Elle !

He laughed loudly, laughed with glee,
But out she came and in he went,
And now, as his last gasp was spent,
He knew *qui*
Est-ce qui rit: elle !

She laughed last and she laughed well,
Until her mirth was so intense
She lost her plea of self-defense.
And it's in hell
Qu'ils font ensemble des kyrielles.

Peninsular

No MAN'S an island; it is just not Donne,
And even when we're finished and we're dead,
We're still not quite cut off from everyone
So long as we're remembered or are read.

Not yet an island, I am of an age
When one begins to feel peninsular;
And when I put my pencil to the page,
I like to feel my pencil is an isthmus

In which to find a rhyme for Christmas,
Or something that is even tinseler.

Gibbons

WHEN gibbons saw *Decline and Fall*
It nearly sent them up the wall,
And shortly after the abatement
Of that shock, one made this statement:

"As gibbons, we decline to fall;
Indeed do not decline at all.
And only if we find a mate,
Are we inclined to conjugate."

Mnemosyne

HAVE you forgotten me, or have I you,
That you no longer come on cue,
Mnemosyne, goddess synonymous
With memory ? How ominous
It is that you don't keep your promises;
Which now seem more like menaces,
And you've become my nemesis.

Spare me your animus,
Goddess anonymous !
My mind's so lame,
I scarce recall your name.

A Politician

THOUGH he's no longer lauded
His applause will never fail;
He was publicly applauded,
And now he's clapped in jail.

Mites

(Demodex folliculorum)

SUPPOSE they knew, those highbrows,
That something diabolical's
Rooted in their eyebrows
And frolics in the follicles;

They'd be less supercilious,
Indeed, it's almost certain
Their brows would droop as illy as
A fountain there's no squirt in.

Did the high and mity know
That they were lodging mites,
It would give them vertigo;
And they'd forego their heights.

Yet they might not lay low those mites,
However low they laid their sights.

Feet

Behold the lowly caterpillar,
Sometimes still and sometimes stiller
When he stirs he gets him hence
By undulating increments.

The effort of this seems to tax him,
From which fact I draw a maxim
That I think is worth repeating:
Many feet are self-defeating.

It's true the lowly millipede,
For all his feet, can make some speed,
Which shows one can't, in every case,
By counting feet predict the pace.

And yet, as every poetaster
Knows, the fewer feet the faster,
Until you are reduced to one,
For then
You hop,
And cannot
Run.

The Period

Concentrate on the small.
Leslie Mellichamp

I'M ASKED to write of something that is small,
And since the smallest things are myriad,
The choice is very great; but of them all
I think you are the greatest, period.

Without you nothing could be said and done,
And we would be forever lost in limbo,
Nonplussed, regretting that we had begun,
Our mouths agape, our arms disarmed, akimbo;

Or else we'd ramble on, clause after clause,
Slowed only by the comma's little crook,
Or by a semicolon, which gives pause,
But does not take us wholly off the hook;

Most pointed of all marks of punctuation,
Your littleness belies your ultimation.

A Four-footed Metaphor

A METAPHOR'S a thing
Half métamorphosed;
A figment that is ming-
gled, recomposed.

In the zoo, the other day,
I mét a four-foóted metaphor,
Half man, half horse, and heard him say,
"It's true I'm less free than before,

"And forfeit are my footloose ways.
But in the zoo I find more action;
I'm admired, I find it pays
To be the centaur of attraction.

"For I am more centripetal
Than any satyr such
As has two legs, capripedal,
And cannot stirrup much."

Clothes

IN SHAKESPEARE'S plays
Nobody knows
For days and days,
Till the very end,
His closest friend
If he's changed his clothes.

Prospero has
But to put on his hat
And he's what he was,
A duke, like that !

They gladly aver,
Who knew him before,
"You are what you were
When you wear what you wore."

Fireflies

...like a glowworm in the night,
The which hath fire in darkness, none in light.
Shakespeare, *Pericles*

IT'S ONLY when it's getting dark
That fireflies are seen to spark.

Donc
C'est seulement quand arrive la nuit
Qu'on voit la luciole qui luit.

Und
Man sieht nur nächtlich, als es dunkelt,
Wie der Feuerkäfer funkelt.

But
In Britain fires don't flit, and so worms
Must suffice; they sing of glow-worms.
(While the male glow-worm can fly,
His light's too cryptic to descry.)

In every clime excessive light
May sometimes keep things out of sight,
And they keep out of sight who know
That in the light they have no glow.

Polka

I KNOW that it takes two to tango,
Two again for a fandango;
Sixteen are best for a quadrille,
More, really, for a Highland reel.

But who can say how many spots
Are needed to make polka dots ?
How to count them ? If one tries,
They start to dance before the eyes;

But then my heart with pleasure trots
And dances with the polka dots.

The Truthsayers

How loudly they once cried
Truths others wouldn't utter;
But now they merely mutter,
Having found upon which side
Of their daily bread there's butter.

Turbyfill

He was anthologized, Mark Turbyfill;
But can he, though he made a stir, be still
Remembered ? At the very most, perhaps he
Might be read as much as Adelaide Crapsey,
Or share a shelf with Clara Shanafelt,
Whose fame's as bare as an iguana pelt.
Only those who've worn a derby will
Be old enough to know of Turbyfill.

Since he'd no use for rhyme, to rhyme his name
Will not, I fear, do much for his acclaim;
And yet I feel my heart superbly thrill
With joy to hear a name like Turbyfill.
It's topsy-turvy as a thurible,
And pungent; would it were more durable !

A Poem Is Nothing

A POEM is nothing if it can't delight
The ear, delight the ear, and not the sight.
It must do this, however much its freight
Of image, thought and feeling give it weight.
And if its weight be wanting, that's no matter;
Far better it be slighter than be fatter.

It may indeed lack reason and want sense,
A thing bereft of any consequence,
And yet be so enchanting it allays
The darkest moments of our dreary days.
If truth be reinforced by rhyme and metre
And alliteration, all the better,

But be advised of this, and mark it well:
A poem's a thing of magic. It's a spell.

Winter's End

THE snow is going soon; it can't endure.
Some will be vaporized, escape in air,
However hard its surface and secure
It seems to be now, gleaming in a glare.

Beneath that carapace it seeps, it bleeds,
Unstaunchably it steeps the depths below;
It gurgitates and gorges, urging seeds
And bulbs, those gulping tubers spurred to grow.

At length the last drifts wane to water, waste
Away and leave but livid patches, streaks
Through which the first green shoots of crocus taste
The air, still chill, while all about them leaks.

Half drowned, a mole crawls from his hole to dry;
And pays his annual penance to the sky.

Le Vent

VENTRIPOTENT, le vent tripote
Feuilles mortes, mégots, journaux jaunis,
N'ayant cure d'en faire le tri;
Tout ce qui rebute fait sa ribote.
Beuglant il rit, meuglant il dit:
Il y va, vous autres, de votre vie !

The Wind

THE wind, a billowbellied beast,
Whirls papers, leaves and butts about;
He has no care to sort them out,
For filth and foulness are his feast.
Growling he spouts, howling he shouts:
Your turn is coming next, you louts !

Connecticut Spring

WHEN the thews of winter thaw
Into the dews of warmer days,
When spring bestrews its hues on raw
And rambling hills, and nothing stays
The strident streams that fulminate
Before they flood the ponds of hollows,
And this season's in full spate,
While all that's left of winter wallows;

Upswelling from its ravages,
Appear the baneful hellebore
And succulent skunk cabbages,
Then, from those depths, we hear once more
The peepers voice their strident cry
To meet and mate and multiply.

Summer

THOUGH some, in winter, hibernate,
Summer seems more slumbrous,
Engaging us to vegetate
As trees become more umbrous.
Winter splinters, summer simmers;
Winter sprints, while summer sags
Like hammocks, where we glimpse but glimmers
Through the leaves; ambition flags.

And as the season gets up steam,
And mildew spreads and all is ooze,
We wilt, with no will but to muse
On seasons that are less extreme;

We dream of spring and fall, which are
More poetical by far.

La Berrichonne

Pauvre chère grande femme ! J'ai pleuré
à son enterrement comme un veau. . .
            Flaubert à Tourguenieff

TOO OFTEN, when the grossly great
Have overtimed their final fate,
Their death, though welcome, comes too late
To give us much to celebrate.

Not so George Sand: when she departed
All but the very hardest-hearted
Wept, and the number of her years
Only multiplied their tears.

We might sift all the sands of time,
In every land and every clime,
Yet never find a sand so pure
As she was, or a heart so sure.

As a child she set beasts free;
When grown, sued for the liberty
Of every Berrichon and friend
Imprisoned for his views, or banned.

She drowned her debts and theirs in ink,
And not a moment did she think
Of fame or fortune, but made merry
All her guests in her native Berry.

Now buried in Berry, the heart of France,
Where she led them in revels, song and dance,
She haunts Nohant, henceforth to glow
In the shadow of her own chateau.

When she departed she was painted
So bright, she was almost sainted;
And even when the paint had peeled,
It was a saint the paint revealed.

Another Green Thought

ITS combers calmed and comatose,
The ocean's now so otiose,
That all its surface seems to be
An empty superfluity.

To see a thing so undefined
Strains even the most vacant mind,
Unless we simply let it be
Until our thinking is at sea;

Until our thinking sinks, till we're
But a cerebric bathysphere,
Which finally bottoms in a balm,
A calm that underlies a calm.

No underflowings supervene;
The mind is mindlessly marine,
And is reduced, by its remotion,
To a notion of an ocean.

A Touch of Midas

ALL that we yearned to touch was turned to gold
When we were in our youth, or so it seemed,
So bright was burnished everything we dreamed.
Though it seems tarnished now, as we grow old,

And as we age, our lengthening of years
Brings out a latent lengthening of ears
That strain and stretch to catch what others say,
But we can't hear until they're forced to bray.

Thus, young or old, there seems to be, inside us,
More than a little of the muddled Midas;
Our youth was gilded, but our hearing's cursed
By that first music-critic, and the worst,

And by those reeds that wreaked, then leaked, his ear-jinx,
The fruit of Pan's inept pursuit of Syrinx.

The Dord of Merriam-Webster
(1934–1941)

POOR dord, so soon to be ignored
And nullified, when someone spied
That it was merely "D or d,"
Abbreviating "density,"
An oversight to be deplored.

But should the word dord be denied
Existence ? Let it be restored !

Let "D or d" then signify
Not "density" but "do or die,"
And by pronouncing it as "dord,"
Its meaning will be underscored:

A word such as a standard-bearer
Might display, a verbal sword
That's undeterred, though born of error.

To Paul Pellisson

(1624–1693)
*Who languished in the Bastille, and
Fed a spider from his hand.*

IT TAKES a tireless and inspired insider
To override the shyness of a spider,
And find it can curtail his lone ordeal
To share with her the flies that share his meal.

Just think how much the trust of that arachnid,
As she crawled on the hand that called her back, did
To mitigate her cellmate's state of mind,
While her small life with his was intertwined.

And it is said that Pellisson, when he
Resumed his life outside of the Bastille,
Throughout his hazardous career did just
As he did in his cell, inspiring trust.

So open was his heart, he'd humanize
Every spider in the court who fed him lies.

Fringes

THERE is a charm in what impinges
On the margins, edges, fringes,
And what's in those outer reaches,
Such as flotsam found on beaches.

We love tints that hint of spring,
The leavings of fall's final fling.
The palest promise of a dawn,
The shadows of a day withdrawn;

Legends that were once alleged,
Flights of fancy scarcely fledged,
Mists arising from the myths
Midwifed among the megaliths.

Novelists find plots in things
They witness standing in the wings;
While it's in sideshows that one peeks
To look for oddities or freaks.

Finding life too fixed and formal,
Some prefer the paranormal;
And become the acolytes
Of cryptic cults and mystic rites.

Others find their mental nurture
In the margins of a future
Heralded by UFOs
That hail from goodness only knows.

A few search corners of the past,
As marginal as all the rest,
And find it fun to forage in
The cellars of our origin.

All seek a margin no less deep,
That fringe of death that we call sleep,
And nothing that's imagined seems
To be more marginal than dreams.

While everything seems more sublime,
Framed by a fringe that's hinged on rhyme.

Naromi

I'VE felt the rampant roaring of the sea
Resound within me like a symphony,
And yet I find this woodland brook's small burble
Has more to say to me; it is more verbal.
Who'd not admire such murmerings as these
That make their soft reply to tongues of trees?

As, in Damascus once, a fountain's trickle
Quickened my ear, my heart, to hear it tickle
The quiet of the courtyard where I stood,
Secluded from a clamorous neighborhood.
Such summonings come nearer, clearer, crisper
When they traverse a silence in a whisper;

And we, responding to a muted message,
May feel it has the power of a presage.

A Pocket Globe, ca. 1770
("Showing the latest discoveries")

I HOLD a globe, an orb that's small,
No larger than a cricket ball;
Reduced so anyone might look
With ease upon the track of Cook,

New world and old are here contracted
By Cook's travels, re-enacted
On the surface of a sphere
That makes all distance disappear.

Thus scaled down to a cricket ball,
They come within the grasp of all;
To sail around the world's no trick, it's
Like a run between the wickets.

How prophetic ! In our day
It's almost come to be that way;
For now the world has grown so small
It does seem like a cricket ball !

Not much more than two centuries
Have passed since Cook explored the seas,
And since he sailed, such is our pace,
We spurn our world and yearn for space.

A Philadelphia Dentist
(1875–1953)

I

To BE a dentist was an afterthought;
He trained to be an artist at the start,
And could have been an expert forger, but
Wound up by forging teeth instead of art.

He lacked an artist's temperament, and crime
To him was no temptation; one supposes
He might have been a preacher. His spare time
Was spent in prayer or cultivating roses.

Suppose, however, he'd pursued that art,
That art in which he was so well apprenticed;
I try in vain to cast him in that part,
A part of which yet served him as a dentist.

How light his touch, how artfully he'd spare
The pain of carious patients in his care !

II

THE care of patients quaking in the chair
Was spared him after half a century
In which there was no tooth or denture he
Could not repair and ease, but his own wear,
When he retired, was quite beyond repair.

For two or three more faltering years he fumbled
With a brush and faced a canvas, where
He sought his former craft before he crumbled,
Recalling those with whom he'd been acquainted
In his youth, in graves long overgrassed,
Among them Eakins, whom he almost sainted.

Although he felt outdistanced and outclassed,
I'm pleased to think that, at the last, he painted
Himself into that corner of his past.

Rainbow

A MIST'S not always a mistake,
For it, dividing light, delights the eye.
Glass walls do not a prism make
More radiant than a rainbow in the sky.

However far or faint, that spectrum
Fires the words of any strolling lyrist
Who plies a pen instead of plectrum,
Inspired to poetize when skies are irised.

It is my choice, that moist mirage,
Which draws one nearer, but is never neared,
To be my goal, to be my *hajj*,
The pilgrimage by which I'm steered.

And as I go, the sun behind me
Refracts, attracts, and yet it cannot blind me.

To the Magna Mater

RAISE up a temple, that within it we
May once again behold the Magna Mater,
The dark-maned, many-named divinity
Who reigned until the western world forgot her.

What antique incantations and what mantras
Can we invent to chant to that enchantress ?

Lead lowing herds to yield their milk for Hathor,
To whom the pharaohs first made sacrifices;
Appoint a priesthood to prepare her path or
That of her successor, mighty Isis.

Lift high the lyre, inspire its strings to play a
Hymn to her who reared and rescued Zeus
By tricking treacherous Time, the goddess Rhea,
And let your praises to her be profuse.

For Rhea's second self, Cybele, fierce as
She may be behind her brace of beasts,
Begin the dance with drum and brandished thyrsus
In celebration of her frenzied feasts.

What antique incantations and what mantras
Can we invent to chant to that enchantress ?

Pygmalion

How often that for which we languish
Once it's granted, turns to anguish.

Thus the sculptor, wishing stone
Into a maid of flesh and bone,
Might be dismayed and not escape
A charge of statutory rape.

If only she had seen a palette
In his hand, and not a mallet,
She'd have welcomed him, not yelled,
When she beheld the thing he held;

If she had been portrayed in paint,
Her fear of him had been more faint;
Had Pygmalion used pigments,
All her fears had been but figments.

She would not reverberate
With all those blows she'd come to hate;
But would instead recall how smoothed
Beneath a brush she'd been, and soothed.

While, as it was, she'd feel what pain
She would endure if struck again;
She'd been but slimmed by him who hews
Till then, but now her skin would bruise.

No wonder then, if it might shake her
To be wakened by her maker !

A Phenomenon

IN HIS own day, Shakespeare was held to be
Too natural and too unscholarly;
They praised him, but their warmest praise was cooled
Because he seemed so careless, so unschooled.
While nowadays our education's such
We think his not too little but too much,
And thus deny him any praise whatever,
In favor of some noble deemed more clever.
How strange that, in our democratic age,
We should presume a nobleman more sage
Than such a one, whose native inspiration
Could never be explained by education.

Shakespeare is something else, but not one whom
Some other paid to be his nom de plume.

Dreamlands

I LOVE the lands of Is and Oz,
And Cocaigne, Mu and Camelot.
And every place that never was,
And, sadder still, is not.

No Baedeker describes their bounds,
They're scarcely found on any map;
But when, in dreams, I make my rounds,
Their loss would leave a gap.

Their loss would leave a gap so wide
I'd have to re-invent
Another land, but one inside
Of which none ever went,

And none would ever go, because
It wasn't Is and isn't Oz.

Crows

WHAT call have daws to dawdle, every dawn,
Beyond my window, as they rid their craws
Of scabrous cries to goad the fragile gauze
Of dark that shrouds my sleep till it is gone ?

I rise and shut the window on their shouts
And groping back to bed, I hope it screens
Me somewhat from their raucous whereabouts,
But any sleep is now beyond my means.

"What's lost at dawn is not retrieved at eve,"
I moan: "Why must crows voice their screams
As though they would make carrion of my dreams ?"

Until I'm up for good they will not leave.
Then, when I ask them why, they do not pause
But fly away and cry, "because, because !"

C'est l'ENNUI !

WHAT Baudelaire deplored was boredom;
He deplored it more than whoredom.
And it's true much good has gone
Down the drain that is a yawn.

And true it is that men have warred
For little more than being bored,
Not to speak of civil crimes
Too uncivil for my rhymes,

Though other things may sorely vex
Us, not the least of which is sex.
And what dark thoughts assail the mind
When sex and boredom are combined !

Indeed I think perhaps that may
Be what the poet meant to say.

Above It All

THE hope of happiness to come
Is apt to make some people glum;
They fear they've lived their life in vain
If they've let joy alloy their pain.

The puritan is vexed to see
All vestiges of ecstasy,
And thinks if he will spurn it, he
Will earn it for eternity;

For only when one's on a cloud
May any folly be allowed.
Once there, though, he would still look down
On that on which he used to frown.

While most of those aloft are too aloof
To think how we behave behooves reproof.

Be Oblique !

DON'T be plain, but be oblique;
Skew your words to make them newer.
Don't spell out your meaning, eke;
Place obstacles round which to peek,
Or else you won't find a reviewer.
You must hide or he won't seek.

There's no merit in revealing
What a poet's not concealing.
But, if you make reviewers guess
Your point, they'll share in your success;
And you in turn will find a place in
Their own self-congratulation.

Are you convinced ? I'm not quite sure
I've been sufficiently obscure.